The lucky star of hidden things

Afric McGlinchey

2013

For Laura —
Lovely to meet you
at the Ben Kely
weekend — thanks
for your support!
Warmest, Afric

salmonpoetry

Published in 2012 by
Salmon Poetry
Cliffs of Moher, County Clare, Ireland
Website: www.salmonpoetry.com
Email: info@salmonpoetry.com

ISBN 978-1-908836-08-3

COVER PHOTOGRAPHY: *Michael Ray*
COVER DESIGN: *Siobhán Hutson*

Salmon Poetry receives financial support from The Arts Council

We began as wanderers, and we are wanderers still.

CARL SAGAN

Acknowledgements

Acknowledgements are due to the editors of the following publications in which some of these poems, in their current or previous incarnations, have appeared: *Moth, Southword, Poetry Ireland Review, The Asylum, New Mirage, Revival, Wordlegs, Bare Hands, Under the Radar, The Scaldy Detail*, the *Sunday Tribune* and the *Irish Independent*.

'Late' was commended in the 2011 Magma Poetry Competition, 'Dessert' was nominated for the 2011 Pushcart Prize, 'Scraps' was long-listed in the Fish Poetry Competition 2011, 'Invasion' was highly commended in the Dromineer Poetry Competition 2011, 'Fish plates and star jumps' was awarded second prize in the Chapter One poetry competiton 2010, and 'Do not lie to a lover' and 'Under the heart, a horseshoe shape' won the Hennessy Emerging Poetry Award in 2011.

As Carl Sagan said, 'To create an apple pie from scratch, you must first invent the universe.' This apple pie wouldn't have come together without the support of many fellow poets and family, including John Fitzgerald, Donal Gordon, the Bishopstown writers' group, Hibernian poets, Paul Casey, Niall Thomas Murphy, Marie Coveney, Paula McGlinchey, Adam Wyeth, Lisa Burkitt and Denise Blake. The author also wishes to thank Derek Mahon, Paul Durcan, Paul Perry, Leanne O'Sullivan, Jessie Lendennie and Siobhán Hutson.

for Micaela and Cian,
and for Michael, fellow traveller in this universe, and my best critic.
Thank you for making it all worthwhile.

Contents

Sadalachbia, or *the lucky star of hidden things*, is a green star that appears in spring, signaling the end of hibernation and prompting nomads to move their tents to new pastures.

In my dreams I travel home to Africa

Birthstone

My father lays them on the table,
offers me first choice.
Its light seduces: from every angle,

lightnings glide,
a compass with forty norths,
captured star.

I think of its birth, deep beneath
the Drakensberg,
then slipstreamed west

to the long Namibian shore,
deposited on pocket beach,
bedrock gully,

wind corridor; later,
hand-picked by smugglers.
An impulse to possess

this tear of the gods; now my legacy.
Neglected during conflict days,
almost, as with you, abandoned.

I recall those last weeks,
laughing at childhood memories,
taking your hand on a hospital bench,

twisting the ring on your too-thin finger.
I twist it now, on mine,
twirl my tongue over its cool surface,

until it sparks a different view −
and something in its light, a fleck,
reflects you back.

Yesterday, today and tomorrow

In my dreams I travel home to Africa…

…to the heat of early morning Harare,
hustle of the Sunday market, Shona handshakes,
loose and triple, palm to palm;

where buses zig-zag pot-holes
big and black and bold enough to jump into;
white-robed worshippers gather under trees;

chongololo queues wait for pirate taxis;
men, dark as squid ink, drink *chibuku*,
women, wrapped in java prints,

with swaddled babies, rock their backs,
sell plump bananas on laid-out sacks,
or sun-warmed avocados, each ample as a breast.

There's the pin-thin whine of mosquitoes,
then the silence – just before they bite;
drums beating bass into the pavement;

mbiras, jumpy, rhythmic;
voices calling *mangwanani*, *mushi sterik*;
cracks of thunder, clatter of blinding rain;

Willards chips, pungent, red-powdered;
tongue-curling kapenta; *sadza nyama*, hand-rolled;
Sparletta cream soda, green fizz in my nose;

melting tar and diesel fumes; dusty air,
burnt grasses of the *vlei*, heavy-scented petals
of yesterday   today and tomorrow.

Dancing in the moonlight

Barefoot
in banana groves,
your sugar cane weapon
slices juicy-stem rhododendron.
Warm air graces our flamenco.

In the pool, we sway and swirl,
first, a tango,
then, no longer a pretence,
but an opening –
palm to palm.

Water-shaken
we pad to the *rondavel*,
and you smile
as I fall
into your dance.

The water bearers

Far below the ragged track,
purple shadowed,
the river flows.

Three kids
pass bony cattle slanted
on the mountain, clinking bells.

Across the valley, mothers
lean to pluck tomatoes
for the day's main meal.

The children reach the clear, cold,
rushing river, where highland trout
flick yellow-silver glints in early sun.

They scoop and chatter, fill *jagoobs*;
twenty minutes to the river's edge –
a full two hours, barefoot, home.

The sun climbs with them as they wind
the track, like knitting wool,
around and up, and up, around,

no glance left or right at monkeys,
palms or clouds; water's weight
on steady heads and aching necks

– but arms swing free, as they sing and whistle
all the way uphill, to swept yard, pot on fire
and soon, their *sadza* porridge.

After the sand storm

I stir the dust of an eclipsed city,
watch a flight of pink flamingos.
From their midst, a loner
drifts over this sandpit street.

Watch, a flight of pink flamingos;
like the potpourri of abandoned possessions
drifting over this sandpit street,
where I unearth a history.

A potpourri of abandoned possessions,
left while a population took flight.
I unearth a history,
sifting, like flour, old memories.

Left while a population took flight,
a muddle of linen drifts and collapses.
I sift, like flour, old memories,
pitying, twisting, lamenting.

A muddle of linen drifts and collapses,
shrouding this death on the Skeleton Coast.
Pitying, twisting, lamenting,
I stir the dust of an eclipsed city.

Tokoloshe sequence

1

Late

They call us
in the *tokoloshe* hours

to take mrs jimmy
to have her baby

but mrs jimmy has already
had her baby

by the creaking gate
where the cattle come in

grief-witted, arms tight
as rope, she rocks;

baby fingers curl in the dirt,
pale as a bleary sun

ll

Exorcism

Tokoloshe, tall as your knee,
they tell me
showing the whites

of their rolling eyes.
N'anga,
what vision is this?

The oldest shape, he says,
which maddens the mind
to a moult.

A crowd-stilled silence
for the preparation: zebra tail,
ritual mask, skins.

Then – eerie incantations,
at each *rondavel* entrance;
sudden lashed whip, blood tipped.

The sky swells and reddens
into the belly of their terror
– and they flee

pandemonium crushing rib cages,
as *tokoloshes*
emerge from doorways.

lll

Curse

I felt a jolt:
locks of hair, a bone,
bloodied feathers

woven to a snatch,
bound with grass,
hung above my door;

tossed it, with nonchalance
into the hollow pit
of the fireplace.

*

For twenty one nights
tokoloshes have been chasing me
in the dark,

while I've been
pacing,
swilling flames,

not laughing now,
not certain
that they haven't got to me.

*

Watch for the lull
then you'll know
I've given in.

Counting

I remember how you'd move
among birds of paradise,
sun beating against your back

in the waterless months;
yellow lawn crackling underfoot,
only the pool's small diamonds

promising respite;
your dawn ritual in cerise satin gown,
chlorine canister swinging from wrist.

How you'd count returning herons,
cups of tea, cigarettes; encroaching
darkness hidden in eloquent gaze

as you stroked my arm,
watched me read in the sun.
Now I count: to find

the earth has circled one thousand,
four hundred and sixty times,
around the space you've left behind.

Last conquest

You totter, shaking, to the bath,
bestow, like an ancient king,
a fluttering hand. I lumber you
up and in, no ceremony,
offer you a small gift of soap

and at your dismissal, withdraw
to await further instructions.
Summoned again, I avert my eyes
and brace, so you can rise
to the rim, lean on me,

pause for breath, cheeks glowing
an unnatural red, thinning hair
flustered into wet shapes,
hazel eyes fixed
on some remote kingdom.
Then you heave, a behemoth

surfacing, lift one limb, land,
hold, take an unquiet breath,
then swing the other, strangely
bird-thin, bone-white, over.
When you are restored

to a formal dignity, we stand
side by side in the lift, face
tight-jawed doors, and wait,
sorrow's invasion borne
in a tomb of silence.

Dad's manoeuvre

(for my father)

Even now, when I laugh
at the table, a fear races
through me, recalling

the time we were, all ten
of us, hysterical after a joke,
and a potato caught in my throat

trapping breath, no simple choke,
– lungs, a sealed envelope –
and I seared you

with my tear-stained stare,
until you leap into sobriety
– seconds to spare – squeeze

till it shoots from my mouth, and I
heave in the sweetest breath
alive.

The solace of milk

With the drought comes scarcity.
We take a six-hour drive to rescue three
jersey cows with doleful gaze and shifting feet,

return through heat mirages,
past roadside corpses, until sudden rain
spits up the red dust of our driveway.

They graze our garden; the barrels of their ribs
and chocolate eyes lose that desperation;
bantams wander between slow hooves.

Five weeks on. The pair of us, wife and child, follow him,
trip in long dresses through crackling *vlei*;
the sky in flames now, all around,

like last night's barn-fire, burning every scrap
of our precious cured tobacco. We might have wept,
but for this hoped-for solace.

He's wearing khaki shorts and stetson,
veltskoens, open shirt, carries a stool and pail.
reaches low to his own shadow.

We stand behind her, slightly to one side,
waiting for the white tide.
He glances back from under his hat

without breaking rhythm, coaxing her,
flank pressed by his right thumb;
it issues forth then, in a stream,

and everyone comes running. We heave
along the dusty track, to our back kitchen.
The sunset deepens into cinnamon.

Night scents

I lie in bed,
turn my nose
to the pillow

your memory,
as visible to my nostrils
as the night lamp.

Curtain ushers in butter-
soaked toast, wide-awake lily,
air before storm;

I sense my way
by pheromone,
as hallucinations spill:

saddle sweat, smack of salt, almond;
twang of diesel, turning milk;
from the boiler, burning fur

and I am back there –
steam-cracking tobacco
stalks me, steals my sleep.

In the garden,
eucalyptus,
citrus, spice:

like notes on a piano,
twilight
closing the flower.

He was

a windmill,
endlessly moving, yet fixed

He was a cobra
fangs millimetres from a wrist

He was a crystal decanter,
flung across a room

He was a rain-filled tent
in a monsoon

He was the dragonfly
walking on a sun-baked back

He was a cored apple
filled with *dagga* for a cooling smoke

He was the fishing knife,
held against a *madalla*'s throat

He was an orange
rolled to a rogue elephant

He was the jacaranda drum,
played in an empty riverbed

He was a chameleon,
uncertain whether red or green

He was a motorbike,
swivelling three sixties in a storm

He was a swimming pool
made from a drought-stricken furrow

He was the day after
tomorrow.

No need

No need to tell me
that endings are a moment
of transcendence, and all that is solid
melts into air;
no need to remind me of the eyeblink
tales of life:
like furniture, stacked on the lawn,
that vanishes in a lizard-flick.
No need to challenge me to walk
the high wire, or drag me to a party
with all the wrong people,
where short men take up space
with knuckles on hips,
and there's barely elbow room.
No need to show me I'm in safe hands –
I've seen your scar
and know what you're made of.
No need for you to hold up
a cardboard cut-out sun:
I remember how it looks, how it feels.
Or to suggest that I'm more stone
than heart:
what do you expect?
I'm still half a couple from ark days
pickling memories in a jar.
No need to say that love will return
some day,
like *speech after long silence*;
that's   dirty talk.

Rats

I saw it shuffling along the beam
above the flickering TV, screamed,
threw him the gun, but he said no,
she's carrying a little one, made me wait
until she returned.

'Now, now!' But another hung
from her teeth, as she crossed again. After I'd run
from the room, he watched, as she brought
fourteen of them into our home.
I should have known then.

It was grim, the lifetimes of years,
while I laid poison, knocked them off
one by one, sniffed out grey corpses,
scraped up remains. He accused me
of endangering owls, destroying the food chain.

But the chain being destroyed was the one
that bound me to him. When I awoke one night
to see them scamper across dresser and window-sill,
over our bodies, under the quilt,
I had to kill.

Dessert

So there I was,
lying beside my soon-to-be-ex.
You'd think we could spoon up together,

slide an arm around a waist, just for old times' sex.
I mean sake.
Sex – God forbid! But no, of course we can't.

And now I know why. It's not me.
It's X. Oh yes, the X factor.
Which slipped his mind during that 'I can't go on

any more. I'm starved for love' speech – over dinner.
Funny, that. Being starved for love.
I've been trying to tempt him for the last three years,

with candles, aromatic oils, lingerie – every advance
repelled:'I'm tired. I'm stressed. And now YOU WANT ME
TO HAVE SEX?!'

Suddenly he was buying Calvin Klein and Boss,
had his teeth cosmetically enhanced,
lost weight, picked fights three times a day.

Even with the kids
his laugh
had no lungs.

Because X, of course has five languages
and a PhD, not to mention a hot body.
And I'd bet a million dollars, X isn't a day over thirty.

The truth is, I said nothing. Let him say it all.
You did the main course.
Here's dessert, baby.

Exit

I hide my machete,
speargun, sling,
batwing it out of here

with jackel, polecat, lynx –
no more monkey tricks,
just loose & quick.

White sky

Outside, the sky is white as snow,
but there is no snow in Africa today,
not in Accra, Djabouti, Entebbe,
Addis Ababa or Zanzibar.
It's an impossibility, the idea

of blizzards, gales, aberrations
of winter, while we sit here,
hugging the heat to our pores.
The board flicks names: Brazzaville,
Lilongwe, Kinshasa, Babouti...

Our destination will land us
in the ice-chill, erase
all memory of this temperature,
the slow, langorous sway
of sun people.

                    ★

Umbali wa mwisho wa safari –
Have a safe journey – says my screen.
Newsflash of an earthquake in Haiti –
all over our spinning planet,
weathers, shudders, rocks, cracks.

                    ★

We tip this way and that, curving now
towards Youghal, and already
Africa is melting away, as a caprice of light
flicks up totemic images,
Northern childhood memories.

The road

Free running

for Cian and Nathan

Some may dispute
the possibility
of seven paces

up a cliff-high wall
briefly sky-bound,
then a flick flack back

to ground; or across
from pillar to pillar,
to finger-gripped gutter;

monkey's long
swing to roof flexed
red with pantiles

and chimney pots
but I'm metamorphic –
watch

as I scale it
velcroed runners,
a spider's chitins

up scaffolding
then dive,
rotate mid-air,

a feline,
land, leap
across bonnets

side-spin the lamp post
vault park railings
jack-rabbit-sprint

Sparks

He levers with a wrench,
loose-limbed, speedy,
in oil-stained jeans,
muscles flexed,
fingers dextrous.

Hiss and swing
as an aperture arm
pulls the tyre from its rim,
plucking it first round the edges,
like a high, hard scab off skin.

He climbs to a mezzanine
stack of tyres,
selects one,
throws it down like clay
on a potter's wheel.

The machine pops;
tyre snaps back, clank
of hammer against steel,
then the balancing act,
lid hovering, a raised eyebrow.

He squats, spins the tyre,
buzzes a drill, swivels nuts,
slick as a job at a pit stop.
I reverse, eye in the rear view
mirror, sparks flying

Bodytalk

(for Jane)

Poppy stood beside a chair, her breath held,
one eye studying contours – then, with charcoal,
blind-stroked him in

Annie, wedged in by the sink, spilled water
over wrist, an arm's length from his splayed knee,
blocking the view

Helen turned a slow circle, chose a spot;
small hands lifted to frame diagonals,
Picasso-esque

Yelitza squatted, then sat cross-legged.
With a small easel in her lap, she sketched
full-frontal, stared

Ilse frowned, stabbed markings, punctured body
parts on sheet after sheet, hung on a line,
in denial

Madeleine applauded at the vision
– a man! – then loaded senses, flame and blood,
mouth a quiver

Sonia blackened hair, silvered limbs and chest,
gave him a green-eyed slant, the rest a smear
of streaking red

Pablo found his thunder through angry hands
and weapon poised – articulate, a Zeùs
in transit, fleet

Roisín gave in to thighs, fallen open,
neglected all but the ditch, swatch of black,
a shadow kiss.

Charge of the white paint brigade

The first scrapes of paint
turn floors into grey hills,
evicted ghosts shadowing the walls.

Hope slides into mistrust
of the green-skinned damp; but you
reach for roller tray and brush

and with a mother's mantra
on your breath, stroke
mould-stained surfaces

to smooth lambs of white.
Your assistant is six,
in a star-struck tee shirt;

buck naked underneath,
taut buttocks and tiptoed feet,
the mark of his razor-edged intent.

You check progress, as he drops
to lace the skirting with his signature,
spattering pages, erasing bad news.

Much later, as we celebrate,
the silk-white rooms shine
like sweet-talk.

Fish plates & star jumps

If you stare straight ahead,
you might catch
the lamp post
in your peripheral vision
doing star jumps
in front of
the stopped traffic,
with no notion of itself;

leave your car
in the rain-swept
street! Make your *own*
four-limbed leap,
free of the bars
of our earth-
bound constraint –
your light breathing
over the torrent

of pedestrians
as the pavement collects
puddles of fish,
like spinning
plates,
in a head-patting
tummy-rubbing
moon-mad rain-skin
jam...

'Bodhrán makers suspected as goats go missing'

(news headline)

A wild herd in the moonlight,
last night's eclipse still rimming their minds,

black vault of the heavens
ash-starred.

A bearded billy
flaunts boomerang horns,

does a rock gavotte,
concubines in attendance.

From a van, their musicians' hunger
releases sheepdogs –

a three-way round-up
under night's stern eye,

its blanket streaming nebulae
in their wake.

In Co Clare, the hanging tree,
dark, tugging weights.

A night for stripping skin.

Girl without a horse

(for Micaela)

She searches country roads
until she finds one –
beyond the long-roped goat.

He is unbridled wildness,
the shag of his white coat
brazened with muck.

Her hand opens
with an apple core
invitation.

He shivers, snorts,
bends to the scent.
Then,

blood-warm attention
as she steals to the feast
of his back.

Between thumbs

a wide blade
of grass. I pull
it taut until
the clean green of it
is pin-straight,

flanked by pink;
put my lips
to the paper-sharp edge,
air its siren;
remember how

a good thick blade
whistles long and low;
lighter, lime ones, high
to the ear; some furred
and thick, others cool

and slippery, or waxy
to the touch.
Skinny ones especially
are good for sucking,
chewing the bitter sap.

When was the last time,
I lay under blue
in the cattleless meadow,
measuring clouds
with my spears,

promising myself
I'd never forget
being twelve,
alone,
in a field?

A moment before the rain

Only four remain standing,
refusing to be sheep,
or simply dumber than the rest,

impossible eyelashes
batting
as we walk by.

I eye their udders,
feel a pang
to pull on those teats.

That's unnatural, she said,
Maybelline lashes tremoring
at the thought,

while I lean into
the memory of head-pressed
warmth, the give of her.

I stand in the cold
surge of rain,
contemplate.

On not flicking my tea towel at his departing behind

It's indiscernible really,
the transition between controllable child
and charming, deviant adolescent,
who appears with four friends in tow,
sunburned, after a day's surfing at Inch,
a full three hours away,
but who thinks of time, fuel and distance
when the waves are head-high,
glassy tubes of perfection –
which is why I'm torn between a caress
and tight shoulders at the debris left
in his pursuit of the next activity:
building beer barrels into a house-high
pyramid at 2am, only to tumble down,
chip an elbow, attract a garda warning
and also praise for creativity...
and besides, how can I nag about dishes,
flung-about clothes, mouldy-skinned old tea,
or stinking runners dropped,
when, after his declaration, 'I scored three tries!'
he lifts me up and whirls
and I know he's missing his girlfriend, the one
he hasn't mentioned since February;
and he's nineteen, the age his father was
when he fought in a guerilla war
on the wrong side,
his horse shot from under him;
instead of fleeing,
he fell to his knees and wept;
so, I cherish war-free youth,
forgive impatient hunger,
grab the tender moments.

The road

(for Derek Mahon)

I make my way on a pot-holed road,
weathered, scored in strips of tar
like black ink; with bare feet, read
its braille. My rhythm swerves.
Give phrase and line
more time, you say: 'Each verse
of mine will take a month, a year.'
I read you in the quiet hours, words
weaving light and air; remember.
'Have you ever stood in a lane
and listened to its story?' Stairs creak
as I descend, arrive at the road
again and, walking, close my eyes,
terrified. It goes on for miles.

Eighteen

When I was eighteen,
I swam four lengths underwater;
he kissed me, told me he loved me.

I let him touch my breasts;
walked across the ridge of the sofa
as he proposed.

What would you have been,
my little one, who beat
inside me for five months,

remained nameless, have no grave.
Yet your presence is felt in wordless
whisper, and on this day, in sunshine,

rain, or fog, I listen for you, the hum
of your shape cradled between pelvic bones.
You would be eighteen.

Quest for another hour

(for Aidan)

Summer unrolls
like a sleeping mat,
flat and grey. You sigh
and cast aside your swimsuit,
unwrap your just-delivered kindle,
solace for the holiday not taken.
Wander down the road to read
to Aidan, now he's going blind.
He becomes mythical, tenacious
endurance in his breezy stance.
Glass in hand, he smiles slowly
as you recite a poem about
the fracturing world, that somehow,
by a state of grace, remains
sufficiently intact to spare us
one more hour, or day, or week.

Under the heart, a horseshoe shape

I never met you, danny murphy
but I know you had a child of six
and that christy gave you
mouth-to-mouth and pressed
your chest, and when the ambulance
came, they continued for an hour

and your phone
rang in your pocket
someone called kath
and I imagined
a planned date
and you, late

and I imagined your future,
trampled out of existence
in the space of a car turning
in the space of a horse rearing
in the space of the sun sinking
below the hill

The gate

(after Derek Mahon)

They need a context, to eke out
their distant echo, undisturbed by cities or freeways,
some place desolate perhaps, where bones
have settled well below earth,
and bats hold on in the favoured dark,

where a fox might bark; a place
to find comfort among moth-coloured shapes
in the unlit gloom,
haunted by the passing
of a stranger at a gate, its brittle

metal rocking on loose hinges,
raven-blue grooves indented and weathered;
or a stray, looking for a shelter to coil into,
away from the cooling air;
nature's dissolution shared with human debris,

relic of a blue kettle tipped
to one side and growing moss;
above the cracked mantel,
a thorned heart.
The gate stirs, lifts the torpid air

to a condition of unreason,
and at any moment
they might step across,
feel the weight of this gate
on a solid leaning arm.

Evening draws in,
darkness creeping closer,
until the gate is all there is,
and even that a shaky prospect,
disintegrating under seeping ink.

The night glides its wings,
silent as an owl,
only the wind to attend those ghosts,
knowing there is something they need to say.
The air curls round mounds, trees, stones,

like little leaves, to carry sorrows,
secrets, lost dreams.
An unlocked gate shudders,
creates a breach,
invitation to leave.

What we saw

Seeing

Yours is not the same as mine.
Perhaps I see wet streets, broken-
spoked umbrella left on a step,
dripping dress on a line; while you,
looking in the same direction, might see
a crossed leg, the way the earth
cradles a park bench, red flare
of a running child's hair,
grandiloquent gestures
of a deaf couple
at a pavement café.
Maybe we both see the old man
puffing his pipe in a doorway,
smoke-waves fibrillating
his astonishing eyebrows.
Bombarded by details
– stark, lavish, unruly –
we record with our camera-eye
those which harmonize
with our mood of the moment,
symbiosis of feeling and seeing.
A trick of the mind, selection necessity.
Light pulses in, we blink, and images
race along our cortex, generating
attraction, perception, connection.
In youth, our sight is more brilliant,
blurring indistinct with age;
light dims,
the eye shifts inwards,
to the dimension of memory.
A blind, different kind
of seeing.

All roads

(a found poem)

One thing you should know is I'm a whore
on the beach at Pampelonne, where the sea
is milky white, barely distinguishable from
the early morning sky. How right you were,
Pascal, about our inability to sit in a room
alone! In the silence of my third-floor
attic under the mansard roof, I was faced
with the tedium of my existence. I set out
on a journey, praying that the road would
be long. He appeared beside me, spindle-
shanked, beach-blond, gave me courage,
palm touching the black lace of my bodice.
His name was Santiago. Our baskets grew
more intense as we were mobbed by heat.
We followed others, grapepickers and brick-
layers, computer programmers and sex
workers, these and millions more, my
ancestors, who wandered in the wilderness
for forty years. The stars came floating down
like paratroopers. We who saw, hushed;
the noise stopped abruptly, as though a
fountain had been turned off. Then, he was
gone. They were gone. I was alone on the beach
at Pampelonne, where the sea is milky white,
barely distinguishable from the early morning sky.

Scraps

It has been drifting in icy tides,
feathers peeling,
like stitches unpicked

from a mucky cloth,
dangling from the lip of a wave
before dipping below water.

Our rudder rubs against
the skinny corpse – to find its life
not quite extinguished.

Further out, we discover others;
a trio, clustered
up against a rock,

butting bodies, beaks and orange legs;
scrambled concoction
fetched up by the slick.

A quiet curse.
Bent heads droop over the side,
trail nets, scoop flesh.

There is no rescue. Just silence in a boat
in the black heave of water,
men and their staring eyes,

reaching with a boathook;
one holds my arm, while I film:
collecting scraps.

Burial

(for Kay)

She chariots them across the lawn,
souvenirs, effects,
wheelbarrows them to a grave.

Mandolin, birdcage, leatherman,
heeled into the dark space.
She chariots them across the lawn.

She would throw her heart in,
but it's too heavy
to wheelbarrow into a grave.

A chest filled with relics, scraps:
iMac, artwork, egg of an ostrich;
she chariots them across the lawn

to this mercy pit for memories;
anchoring them, like his body, to earth;
wheelbarrowed into a grave.

Shadows fall on a hill of stones,
tumulus to lay over a life.
A chariot, a cross, the lawn,
wheels, barrow, a grave.

Red letter day

(i.m. three unknown refugees)

Sky and light
from this height
so startling and clear

Tied by tribe
and fear,
they stand on the ledge

choose a final freedom –
fly through a hundred
feet of air

catenated by the wind-
slowed red tape
of final warnings,

to slip
the net closing in
on their safe haven.

All that's left,
dusty footprints
on a window sill

torn safety net
fluttering
on Red Road.

Darkness
wraps round
a Glasgow morning.

Did the outweighed sun
close its eyes
for that brief moment?

Invasion

I can prove to you
that the white raven
does exist,

in a cemetery
between two pillars
strung with nettles,

its pale mirage
shuddering
under a snowy shroud.

And who can blame
its secrecy, when the church
path is bombed

with hob-nailed boots
and camera clicks
and even dandelions rise

for a helicopter view,
swing their clocks
into blinded eyes?

What's more, from a satellite,
I have seen a girl
in south Sudan

walk a thousand miles
with only insects
for food, then deliver

an infant in the desert.
Lizards crept from under rocks
to watch.

She talked to stars, reckless,
their light, an oasis to cling to
through sheets of night;

through howls and sweat — yet
when I flew there, found a caravan
to lead me to her,

she passed the cool mouth
of my camera,
growled her rejection,

glassy as a prophet
drumming omens
in the sand.

On the soles of their feet

I watch it, this Harare life
that I have left: new hair extensions,
heels and shiny faces – *'maybe they're all models
or HIV hookers'*; the guards, with their batons,
guiding white Mercedes between parallel lines;
potholes filled up hourly by street kids
who rob red bricks from suburban garden walls;
dark windows that roll down, float
dollar notes for school fees.

The Book Café is closed, for fear
of revolutionary activity,
and Mannenburg's is shut down too –
all that jazz is quite suspicious.
The black streets rock
with drunken combis; restaurants
have sprung up in the tranquil gardens
of private homes, and look,
there's furniture, clothing, trinkets.

On New Year's Eve, the town is empty;
everyone's headed to Vic Falls,
taken off for Mozambique. But in this bar,
to an African beat, hips and buttocks sway boisterously.
A Roman candle spurts for half an hour,
like sporadic, bent-over laughter. Rain brings frogs
and lulls the crickets, and scents swirl in and then
there's no electricity. You'd think there was a war,
or sudden peace, for all the expectation.

The drive across an unlit town,
son riding shotgun for protection.
A pre-dawn skinny dip among the frogs.
No lights; no water from the taps.
A solitary plane at the airport. But there are diamonds
and cutters and polishers and smugglers
and dealers right next to Econet and Buddy.
There are diamonds.
There are diamonds and bodies.

No banquet for old men

Perhaps I have always lacked
the capacity for rapture;
do they think of this,
the women I have known?
Even when I burn,
I don't sing.

Now, I take to the dark –
an old man clambering
over a young woman's body
is ludicrous and ugly, less
a Handel opera than the flat,
tinny slap of banjo strings.

Nevertheless, heedless
of bowed shoulders
and skinny shanks,
potential ridicule,
I rush to prolong
the banquet of the flesh.

The dog tied in the yard
can smell my thoughts
as I watch the young girls pass.
What are we but beasts of prey,
when all that doesn't age
is the venom of desire.

Wolf House

Like a constellation, they stand
transfixed around him,
she dancing as he plays

piano through the night.
Hot star, blue giant,
he is luminous in the dark,

ready to ignite, each act
performed to a full house,
until darkness has fled

and sunlight stuns them
to sleep. Left with the dregs
he coaxes: 'I can't sleep

now – stay with me', voice
slippery with alcohol,
his left eyelid drooping

like a fixed wink;
those liquor-surreal
hours making her

waver to a nebula.
A rising star, so like him;
his gaze fused on her,

a corpse flower bloom
in a wolf house.
It's no wonder she fled

and he lost his sunlight.
Now, the house
is pitched   to starless.

Shotgun
(for Kate)

We drive down forest roads,
branches scissoring the sun,
into the green depression,

silence punctuated by the crunch
of crisps in the back.
It's a surprise, he says.

I wonder at his knuckled stress,
sideways smile that slides
and swerves.

My hands hold
the bluebells we've picked,
but I am trigger-tense.

Trees clear to a building –
a cross, two friends
at the entrance, a robed priest.

He offers his hand, as though
I am a bride; aisle, lined
with white bryony; the bluebells,

my bouquet. 'Do you ...?' the priest intones.
What can I say?
'I do.' Then, a crash.

My son has dropped
his gun. Catching his hand, I run,
run, refusing to look back.

Dammed

Cot-trapped by the accident of a dropped clock;
momentarily, a low pulse sings.
I am felled, yet uninclined to dread.
Rapt instead with possibilities —

but your time-is-fleeting attitude checks my plea.
You leave. The latch holds back my sob.
I throw sheets over balcony railing
to the *son et lumière* of city street

and searchlight moon — sniff bruised air,
the slime-green stink of riverbank,
gaze at my falling dreams
as they tumble into the pavement.

Above me lies a vast black space
trailing an abandoned veil.

The lucky star of hidden things

Not all journeys begin at the hatching place;
some start with a star's green tip
pointing towards
the river.

Dreams are a bull's eye
swallowed in a shallow cup,
a diamond spray
around the horse's girdle.

She remembers winter's deprivation;
takes three ribs and a whip,
leaves them at the foot
of the behemoth.

She cracks eggshells –
with her out-stretched wrist,
sets them, like miniature water jars, in the desert.
Thirst-slaked camels stand in lines.

She raises her tent
on the freshening pasture,
waits for a warrior. And why should she not
know solace?

When he appears,
trailing footprints in the dust,
she will lead him
to the hidden things.

Leaning into your world

Do not lie to a lover

but on the other hand,
do not always
tell him the whole truth;

sometimes your secrets will feel
like a fire beneath your skin,
silently burning, but they should

be revealed only when required,
like a cat's eye necklace
on a dark road.

Disclosure exposes,
creates a stalking fear
like that of the grasshopper

who sang all summer
and now faces winter
without provisions,

as the wind whoops and fleers,
and sleet skitters over
the whitening ground.

On hold

Feel like I've been put on hold
only no one has told me,
and there's no soothing music…

Wonder whether to hang up
because there's no line to your cave
…nothing but silence…

Maybe your happiness graph
has plunged, like a frozen swallow
dropped to your feet from the sky,

because winter's window is bleak,
and you've withdrawn
your last ten euro from the ATM

and you're looking down at your body
in the shower, missing the jet-rush
of new romance, first time sex.

But that blonde is not going
to make it better, and you know
we're better than this – so

hold on.

Interruption

I am immersed in curves and circles:
lily on a pond; fan of a peacock;
dandelion clock.

They discuss Larkin and Zadie
on the radio, as flames
flute orange notes:

Zadie's Kiki, who forgives infidelity;
Larkin's stone knight
and lady; his doubting

of the nobleman's fidelity.
Loop of a noose
round my credulity...

Yet, the *sharp, tender shock*
of an ungloved hand, clasped
for eternity.

Conductor's baton-swoop;
glass-blower's bloom;
this foetal curl.

I search the fire
for answers
consider   *what will survive.*

Leaning into your world

Yours was an impenetrable loneliness;
a skeletal tree leaning away
from nomadic winds.

I passed
and found arms braced,
like rocks for waves.

Your mouth, skin, hands –
these are my borders now,
my land.

With a knife,
you measure rock pools,
clouds, my hips.

We bump against each other
while walking, laugh at rain,
slide to grass.

Our bodies trapeze
like laundry
cavorting on lines.

A hand held brings tears.
Such a winding memory,
delicate thread.

We sleep when birds sing,
read poems
lifted to light.

I divert misgivings;
a crack in the sky
is just a small thing.

Moving in

Will you have me as I am, then,
with just a laptop and a satchel
and what I'm standing up in?
Will you fall with me to bed
when the small hour finds us,
cast off misgivings,
wake to the impulse of the day?
Will you resist the young face,
attraction of the strange?
My heart can shred to tatters still,
so if you find you're listening
to a greedy ego brooding in the dark,
will you remind yourself
what's fanciful, what's real?

Totems

I have no ogham
to stroke my way back to tribal roots.
No sod of earth

cradling an ancestral rib;
no unicorn standing by a moonlit lake,
or white crow watchful from a treetop.

My totems are a laptop open to skype,
where I lean towards my husky-voiced child,
her virtual presence at breakfast;

Facebook updates: his back flip into a Malawian lake,
cupped palm holding the sun;
half-stripped boys on a kopje, waving bottles;

your wrist, within reach,
the ring you made me;
my pen and notebook, camera,

the trumpet flower
blasting red into my morning;
And on the shelf, your glass,

blitzed with a blue you could
dive into, curved to the shape
you'll touch tonight.

Yes

(after James Joyce)

...yes and then
I touched my finger to his lips
to stroke away the cider,
and put it to mine
and our tongues went plunging
— such a lush sweetness —
the grass so springy-soft on the cliff
and the waves crashing below
and I had to catch my breath
and the night's perfume drowned
that tang of lamb
and I thought of my first kiss
— *what was his name? Johnny?* — *yes,*
his tongue so unexpected,
wriggling like an eel,
but this time it felt different,
and even his silence didn't matter
when he stared, *stared* at my breasts
and I let my hair slip loose
like that Cape Town girl,
and *you have moonlight in your eyes*, he said
so I took him in my hand
and he whispered, would I,
ma petite phalène, he said
and I thought I may as well,
as well him as another,
and the sea was swirling below us in a froth
the sky gorgeous with stars
and I suggested with my eyes
that he ask again
and I knew he would
and I wondered if I'd say yes
and then I urged him down

and he found his way
through all my layers
and I might, I thought, yes
I think I will
say yes.

Glossary

Yesterday, today and tomorrow
the name of a flowering bush common to Southern Africa, on which three different coloured flowers blossom

chongololo   Shona: a centipede common in Zimbabwe

chibuku   Shona: a home-brewed beer, made from maize

mbira   Shona: a xylophone

mangwanani   Shona: 'good morning'

mushi sterik   Chilapalapa (pigeon Shona): 'very good' / 'very well'

kapenta   dried fish

sadza nyama   Shona: maize meal, with meat (nyama). Sadza can also be made into a porridge.

vlei   Afrikaans: marsh

rondavel   Afrikaans: a small round house, with a thatched roof.

jagoob   Slang: large plastic container

tokoloshe   Xhosa: an evil spirit, believed to be capable of possessing people. Many tribes in Southern Africa fear the tokoloshe and believe in its powers.

n'anga   Shona: a traditional healer, who is also believed to have the power to exorcise demons.

birds of paradise
a flower, native to South Africa, which resembles the bird of the same name.

speech after long silence
The title of a Yeats poem

dagga   Afrikaans: marijuana

the day after tomorrow
translation of the word Hwedza, a rural district, and our home (in the old days, if you walked from Harare to Hwedza, you would get there, 'the day after tomorrow')

madalla   Shona: old man (respectful form of address)

kopje   A small hill, usually a rocky outcrop